LET'S EXPLORE THE NORTH POLE

BABY PROFESSOR

EDUCATION KIDS

When we say "North Pole" we always think of Santa, but where really is the North Pole? How Santa lived there? What does it looked like? here are some fun facts about the most mythical place on earth.

So where exactly is the North Pole?

Well, the Earth rotates or spins around an axis. If you were to draw a line at the axis through the center of the Earth, that line would exit the Earth in two places. At the bottom of the Earth, it would exit at the South Pole and at the top would be the North Pole. The North Pole is the northernmost place on Earth.

There are two North Poles. The north terrestrial pole is the fixed point that forms the axis on which the Earth spins. The north magnetic pole, to which compass needles point from all over the Earth-changes daily.

During the winter, the Arctic ice pack grows to the size of the United States. In the summer, half of the ice disappears.

On May 9, 1926, Richard Byrd and Floyd Bennett became the first people to reach the pole by airplane.

There is no land beneath the ice of the North Pole. The Arctic ice cap is a shifting pack of sea ice which is 2-3 meters thick, floating above the 4,000 meters deep Arctic Ocean.

North Pole is not the coldest place in the world.

In the winter, temperatures average around -34 deg C. In the summer it is quite a bit warmer at 0 deg C. This may sound pretty cold, but is actually quite a bit warmer than the average temperatures in the South Pole.

During the summer the sun is always up. The sun rises in March and sets in September. That's a really long day and night!

Polar bears live in the circumpolar north in areas where they can hunt their primary prey, ice seals. The polar bear Range States have identified 19 populations of polar bears living in four different sea ice regions across the Arctic.

Arctic Wolves can walk on the frozen ground due to the way their feet are designed. That allows them to shift their weight around and to keep a good grip. Not only can they stand the very cold temperatures, they don't seem to mind the part of the year when it is dark for both day and night.

Polar bears are found across the Arctic. They are most abundant in areas with annual sea ice and productive ringed seal populations. There are five nations with polar bears: U.S. (Alaska), Canada, Russia, Greenland (Kingdom of Denmark), and Norway (Svalbard). Polar bears do not live in Antarctica. Penguins do.

White endangered whales are common in the Arctic Ocean's coastal waters, though they are found in subarctic waters as well. Arctic belugas migrate southward in large herds when the sea freezes over.

Snowy owls can live in the Arctic regions of North America and Eurasia year-round. However, some only stay during breeding and nesting season and then migrate as far as southern states, like Georgia, in the United States. Some snowy owls also cross the Atlantic Ocean migrating between Russia and Canada.

The bearded seal is distributed over all the Arctic. The seal is very rare around Iceland. The wanderers, which usually travel alone, are mostly young animals.

Northern elephant seals are found in the North Pacific, from Baja California, Mexico to the Gulf of Alaska and Aleutian Islands. During the breeding season, they live on beaches on offshore islands and a few remote spots on the mainland.